# DENTISTS' TOOLS

We specialize in publishing quality books for
young people. For a complete list please write

LERNER PUBLICATIONS COMPANY

241 First Avenue North, Minneapolis, Minnesota 55401

# Dentists' Tools

*Pictures by* George Overlie
*Text by* Carolyn Lapp

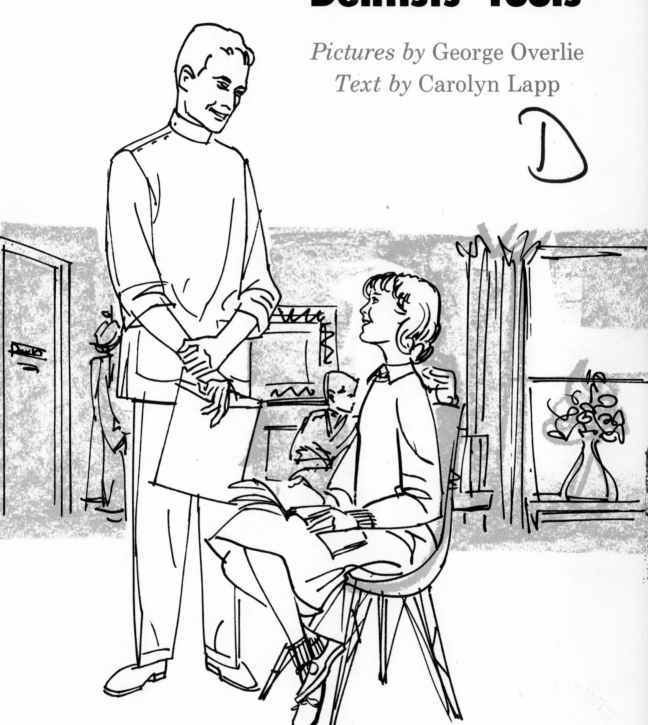

MEDICAL BOOKS FOR CHILDREN

LERNER PUBLICATIONS COMPANY
MINNEAPOLIS, MINNESOTA

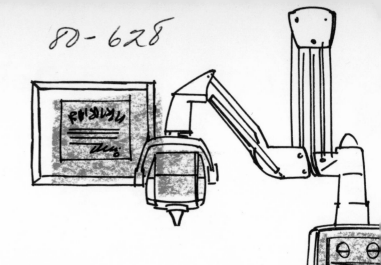

## FOREWORD

There must come to each person during his lifetime a first experience with the dentist. This might occur during his early childhood, or it may be at a later period. However, the earlier it is, and the more pleasant and informative this first visit, the healthier will be the attitude toward Dentistry for the future.

What one hears from others concerning the dentist, their lack of information as to what he does, and the instruments he uses, are often causes of great apprehension. It is the purpose of this book to help minimize the child's apprehension by acquainting him with some of the instruments or tools a dentist uses in his office.

Picturing dental instruments in comic books as demons of torture is obviously frightening to the child patient. In this book dental instruments and equipment are shown with information which should help immeasurably to give the patient confidence in the dentist and knowledge of what may take place in the dentist's office.

HAROLD C. WITTICH, D.D.S.
*Professor, Department of Pedodontia*
University of Minnesota School of Dentistry

1973 Revised Edition

Copyright © 1961 by Lerner Publications Company

All Rights Reserved. International Copyright Secured. Printed in U.S.A.

International Standard Book Number: 0-8225-0010-8
Library of Congress Catalog Card Number: 61-13574

Ninth Printing 1976

TOWEL AND CHAIN

## TOWEL AND CHAIN

When the patient sits in the dentist's chair, a white towel is put around his neck. A chain holds this towel in place. It looks like a large paper napkin and like a napkin it protects the patient's clothing.

## DENTAL MIRROR

A round mirror is used to look inside the mouth. It is about the size of a dime and has a shiny handle. One kind of dental mirror is made of ordinary glass and is a plane dental mirror. With the plane mirror the dentist sees the patient's teeth just the way the patient sees them in a regular looking glass. The other dental mirror has magnifying glass. The magnifying mirror makes everything look larger and gives the dentist a better view of the inside of the mouth.

## EXPLORER

An explorer is a steel tool that is used in examining the teeth. It has a fine point that looks like a bent pin. With an explorer the dentist can find holes in the teeth that must be repaired.

## SCALER

The dentist uses a scaler to scrape away the dirt or crust, called *tartar*, which forms on the teeth. The scaler does the job which the toothbrush cannot do.

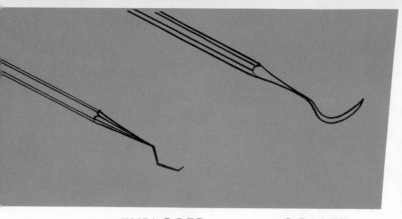

EXPLORER        SCALER        DENTAL MIRROR

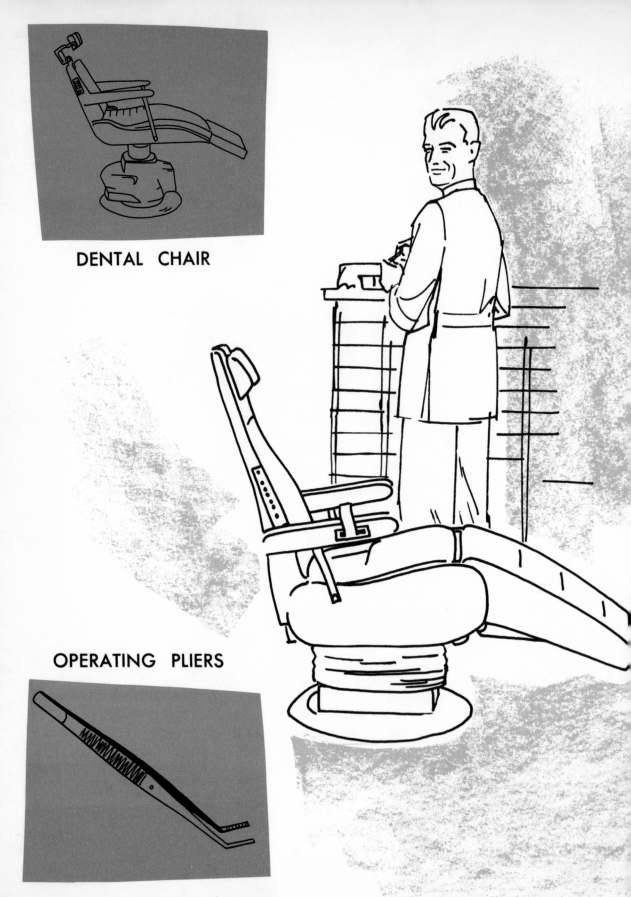

**DENTAL CHAIR**

**OPERATING PLIERS**

## OPERATING PLIERS

The operating pliers are sometimes called tweezers or cotton pliers. They are used to pick up objects that go to and from the mouth. One object that the operating pliers picks up is a cotton roll. A cotton roll is used to protect and keep dry the inside of the mouth when the dentist fills a tooth.

The dental mirror, explorer and operating pliers' are on the bracket table. They are always ready for the dentist when he examines a patient's mouth and teeth.

## DENTAL CHAIR

This chair is very long, almost as long as a bed. But it is curved to fit the curves in a patient's body. The chair has a headrest where a patient rests his head. The bottom of the chair is bent to fit the curve of a patient's knees. The dentist adjusts the position of the chair for each patient. He moves it up and down with electric controls on its side.

## THE DENTAL UNIT

One part of the dental unit is an electric motor. Some of the other parts are: cuspidor, air and water syringes, bracket table, saliva ejector, operating light and Bunsen burner.

## THE ELECTRIC MOTOR OR ENGINE

The electric motor has a handpiece that is attached to an arm. The dentist connects different tools to the handpiece to drill or to clean the teeth. The motor is operated by a foot control.

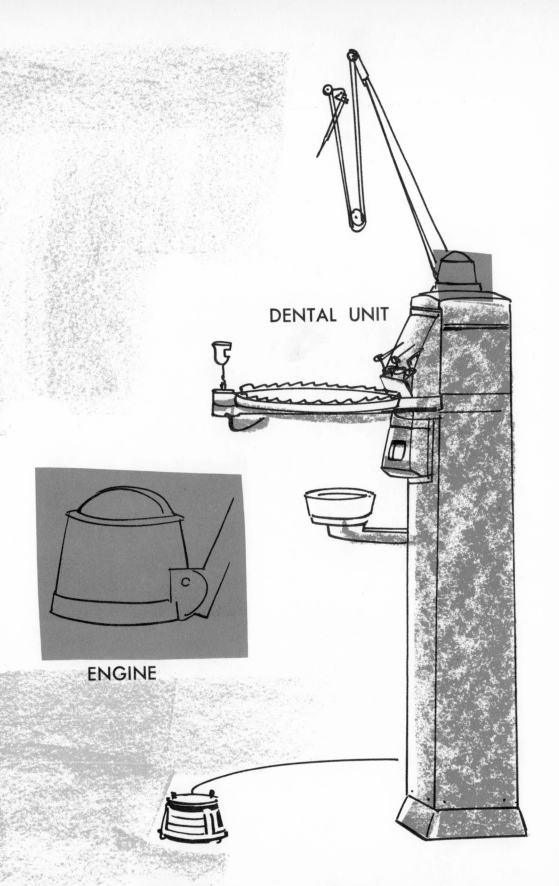

DENTAL UNIT

ENGINE

## DENTAL ASPIRATOR

The dentist uses a small drill to clean and fill a cavity in a tooth. When he uses the drill, a jet of water on the side of it sprays the tooth so that it will not hurt. But the cavity must also be kept dry. To suck up the water from the cavity, and to suck up other wastes in the mouth, the dental assistant uses an aspirator. She holds it in her hand and rubs it gently over the tooth and gums. The aspirator works like a tiny vacuum cleaner.

## CUSPIDOR

The cuspidor on the dental unit is a large round bowl of white glass. A patient spits into this bowl to get rid of the wastes which gather in his mouth. Water runs through a small tube inside the bowl to keep it clean.

CUSPIDOR

DENTAL ASPIRATOR

13

## BRACKET TABLE

A movable arm is attached to this small round table. It holds many of the dentist's small tools.

## SALIVA EJECTOR

The inside of the mouth is normally kept wet by saliva or spit. Saliva is a fluid in the mouth given off by the glands. To keep the mouth dry a small, curved tube or mouthpiece attached to a long hose is used to suck up saliva from the mouth. It is easier for the dentist to work when the mouth is dry. The saliva ejector works like a tiny vacuum cleaner.

## SPRAY BOTTLES

Spray bottles are filled with the solutions that the dentist wants to use for rinsing the mouth. They are kept warm in special places in the unit.

**BRACKET TABLE**

**SALIVA EJECTOR**

**SPRAY BOTTLES**

## OPERATING LIGHT

The operating light is held in place by an arm attached to the dental unit. The arm can be moved around so that the dentist can direct the light to wherever it is needed in the mouth.

## BUNSEN BURNER

The Bunsen burner holds a small gas flame that is used to soften some of the materials needed by the dentist.

OPERATING LIGHT

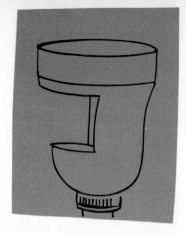

BUNSEN BURNER

## HIGH-SPEED DRILL OR AIROTOR

Some dental units have a drill or airotor that runs at a very high speed. It is called an airotor because air makes the drill turn. The drill sounds like a shrill whistle. While the dentist runs the airotor, water and air are sprayed into the mouth through two tiny holes. The water cools the tooth that might become hot during the drilling, and washes out waste materials.

## BURS

Burs are small cutters made of steel. They come in many sizes and shapes. A dentist uses them to drill and remove decayed parts of the teeth. Burs shape cavities for fillings.

## RUBBER CUP

A rubber cup may be attached to the handpiece. The dentist uses the rubber cup like a toothbrush to clean the teeth. *Pumice* is put inside the rubber cup.

## PUMICE

Pumice looks like powdered toothpaste. Sometimes flavoring is added to give the pumice a pleasant taste.

**RUBBER CUP**

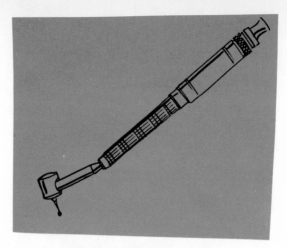

**HIGH SPEED DRILL**

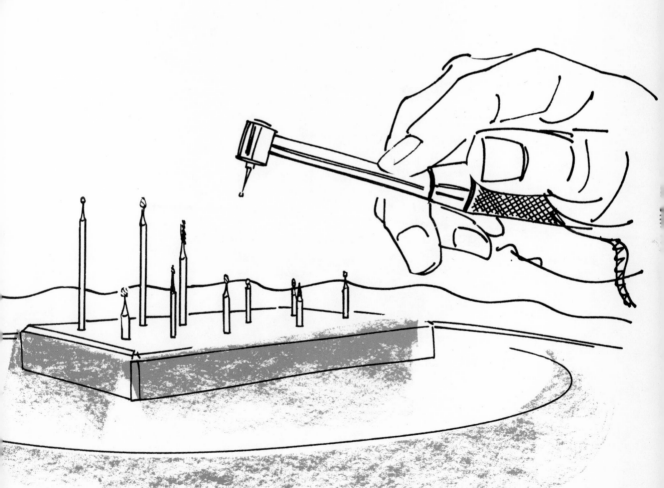

## SILVER FILLINGS

Silver amalgam is the material most used to fill cavities. Mercury and silver filings are mixed together to form a soft mass called *amalgam*. The dentist packs the tooth being filled with the amalgam, which hardens after a few minutes.

## AMALGAMATOR

The amalgamator is a small machine which mixes the mercury and amalgam alloy used to fill a cavity.

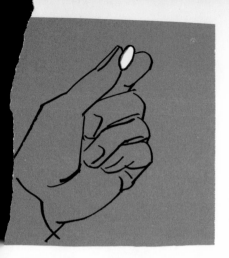

SILVER FILLINGS

AMALGAMATOR

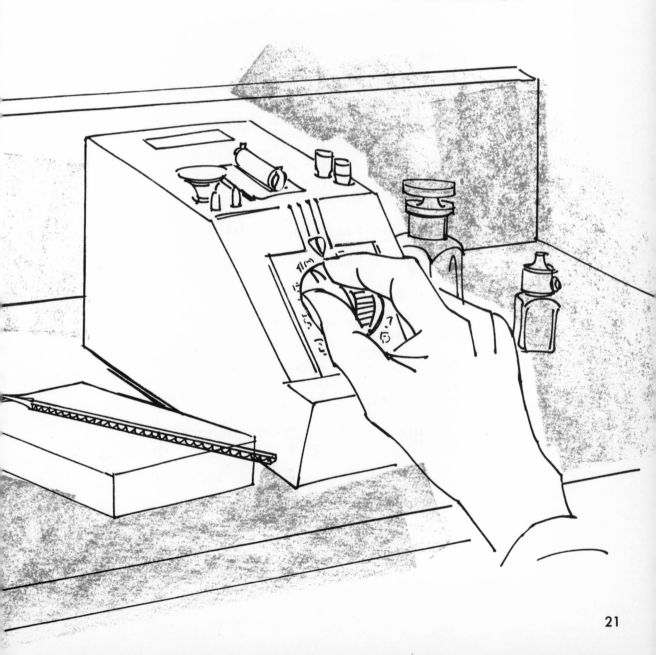

### AMALGAM CARRIER

The filling material is placed into the cavities by the amalgam carrier. It is made up of a tube and a plunger. The plunger pushes the amalgam from the tube into the cavity.

### MATRIX RETAINER

This tool is like a fence or rim. It fits around the tooth that is being filled, helping to hold the filling in place until it hardens.

### PORCELAIN

This is a colorless filling that can be made to match the color of the tooth. It is used for front tooth filling.

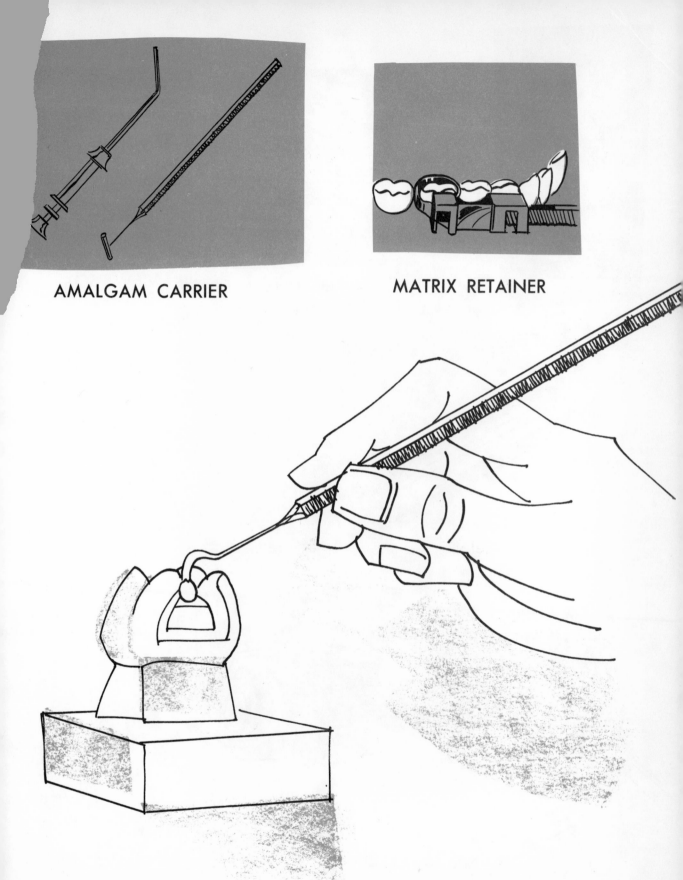

AMALGAM CARRIER

MATRIX RETAINER

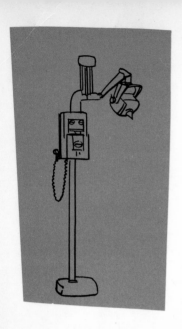

X-RAY MACHINE

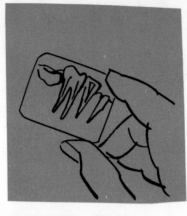

DENTAL FILM

VIEW BOX

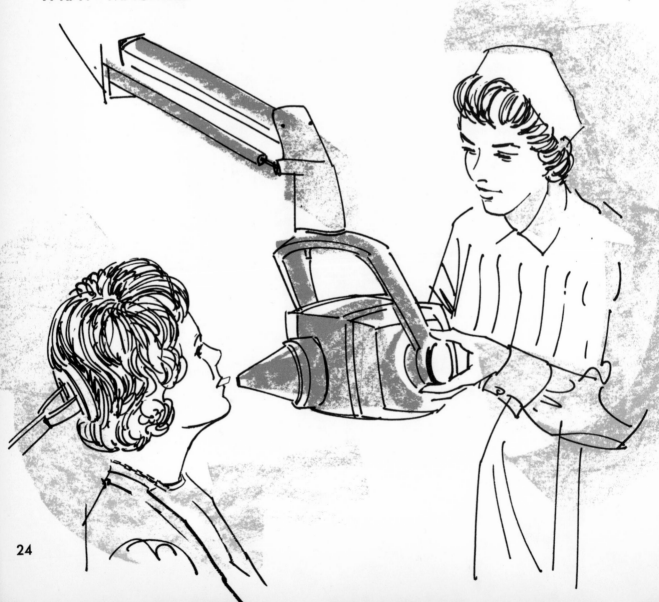

## X-RAY MACHINE

The X-ray machine is used to take pictures of the teeth. The dentist looks at the X-ray pictures to see how the teeth are coming in and to find decay. Wilhelm Roentgen discovered these rays which are named after him and called Roentgen rays or X-rays.

## DENTAL FILMS

The difference between dental and camera film is that dental film is exposed by X-rays and the camera film is exposed by light. Dental film is placed between two sheets of paper like a sandwich. The paper protects the film before it is used. Many of these films are held in place with the finger.

## VIEW BOX

One side of the view box is made of glass. It has a light that shines through the glass. The view box is used by the dentist to look at X-ray pictures. The X-ray pictures are placed against the glass and can be clearly seen when the light shines through them.

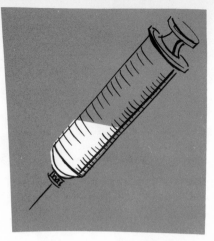

## HYPODERMIC NEEDLE
## AND SYRINGE

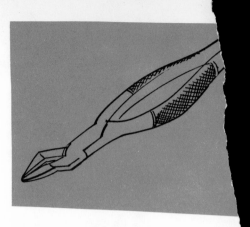

## FORCEPS

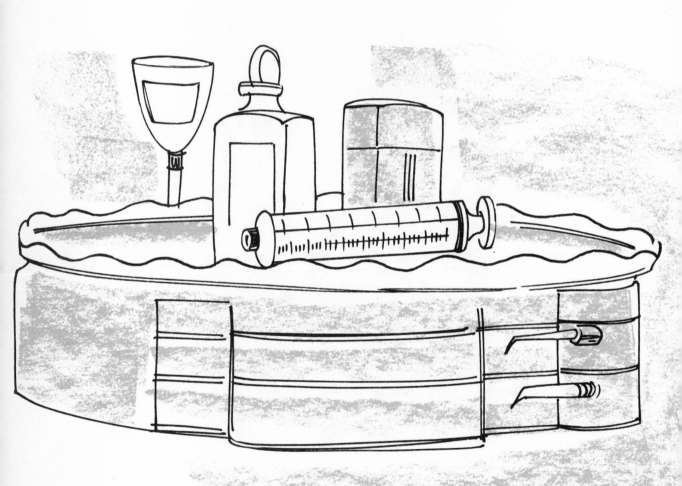

## NEEDLE AND SYRINGE

To give an anesthetic the dentist uses a *hypo-dermic* needle and syringe. The word *hypo* means beneath and the word *dermis* means skin. The needle and syringe are used to inject the anesthetic into the skin or gum.

## FORCEPS

Forceps look like pliers. They are used to pull out a tooth that can't be fixed and must be removed. They are made so that the dentist is able to grip the tooth firmly. Forceps come in many shapes to be used in different places in the mouth.

## ANESTHETIC

The dentist has a special medicine, called an *anesthetic*, that he can inject into the gums. The word anesthetic comes from the Greek word *anaisthēsia*, which means *not feeling*. The anesthetic medicine knocks out the sense of feeling for a short time by numbing the nerves which lead to the tooth being fixed. One kind of anesthetic is called *Novocain*.

BRACES

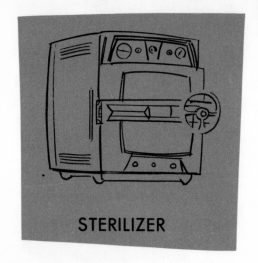

STERILIZER

## BRACES

A dentist called an *orthodontist* straightens crooked teeth by placing braces on them. Braces are wires and bands. Slowly, over a long period of time, the braces guide the teeth into correct position.

## STERILIZER

The dentist uses the same tools over and over. Each time tools are used, they are put into a sterilizer. This is a closed container heated to a high temperature to kill germs.

## DENTAL CABINET

A dental cabinet is a large chest with many small drawers. Each drawer has a different kind of tool or material which the dentist uses.

AUTHOR

**CAROLYN LAPP** attended the universities of Wisconsin and Minnesota and graduated *With Distinction* from the College of Education at the University of Minnesota. Miss Lapp now teaches the third grade at Kenwood Elementary School in the Minneapolis Public School System.

Conscientious in her work, she has always been on the lookout for material that would make the classroom more interesting and enlightening for her young pupils. This led her to *Medical Books for Children*. Thinking that a book on dental equipment would have a place in this series, she set about writing it. DENTISTS' TOOLS is the happy result.

ARTIST

Versatile **GEORGE OVERLIE** does a great variety of commercial illustrations, but he is most happy when working on children's books. He has been a commercial illustrator for more than ten years and is a frequent cover contributor for the *Minneapolis Sunday Tribune Picture Magazine*.

Mr. Overlie studied art in New York City at the Phoenix School of Design and the Workshop School. He now lives with his wife and three children in St. Louis Park, Minn.

When not at work, Mr. Overlie usually heads for the great outdoors and his favorite pastimes — hunting, fishing and camping.